BUDDHISM

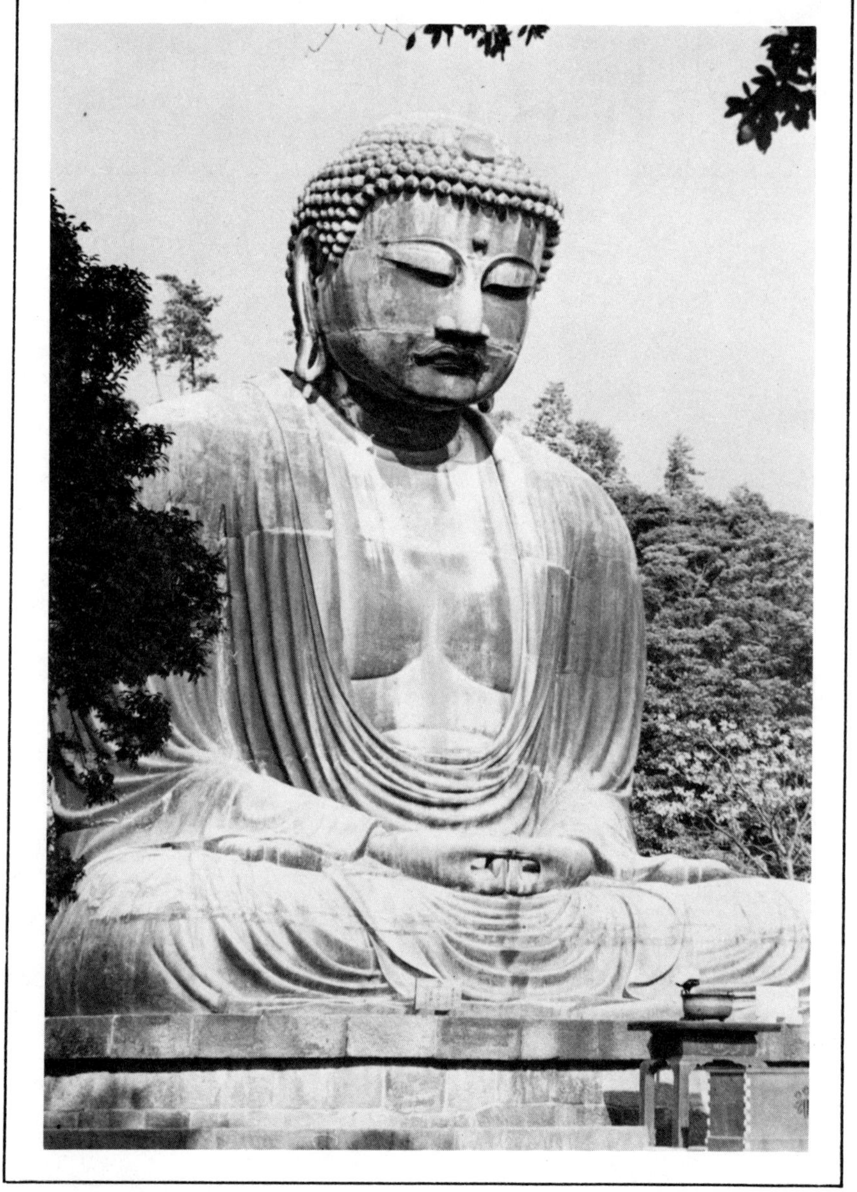

A First Book

BUDDHISM
BY I. G. EDMONDS

Franklin Watts
New York
London
1978

HAYNER PUBLIC LIBRARY DISTRICT
ALTON, ILLINOIS

Frontispiece: a famous image of the Buddha is the Daibutsu, "the Great Buddha" of Kamakura, Japan. This thirteenth-century bronze shows the Buddha in deep meditation, as he may have looked sitting under the fig tree.

Cover design by Beehive Design Studio

Photographs courtesy of: I. G. Edmonds: frontispiece, opposite page 1, pp. 5, 14, 19, 20 (left and right), 29, 32, 41, 54; National Museum, New Delhi; The Archeological Survey of India: p. 24; Metropolitan Museum of Art: pp. 34 (left and right), 44, 53.

Library of Congress Cataloging in Publication Data

Edmonds, I G
    Buddhism.

    (A First book)
    Bibliography: p.
    Includes index.
    SUMMARY: An introduction to the history, principles, and philosophy of Buddhism.
    1. Buddhism—Juvenile literature. [1. Buddhism] I. Title.
BQ4032.E33   294.3   77–12407
ISBN 0–531–01349–9

Copyright © 1978 by Franklin Watts, Inc
All rights reserved
Printed in the United States of America
5 4 3 2

CONTENTS

How Buddhism Began   1

The Beliefs of the Buddha   10

The Spread of Buddhism   27

The Two Buddhisms   31

Other Buddhist Schools   39

Buddhism Today   48

*Important Dates
in Buddhist History*   57

Glossary   59

*Suggestions for
Further Reading*   61

Index   62

The faces on this Khmer tower in Cambodia show Avalokitesvara, "the lord who looks down." The tower has two other faces on the opposite side, so this popular bodhisattva *can see in all directions.*

HOW BUDDHISM BEGAN

More than twenty-five hundred years ago, there was a man who became very dissatisfied with life in India where he lived. He turned to the Hindu religion, but failed to find the peace of mind he wanted. After years of study, he worked out his own ideas of salvation. Using the Hindu religion as a base, he made changes and improvements to create the religion now known as Buddhism. He was called the *Buddha*.

The word *buddha* means "the enlightened one." *Enlightenment*, in the Buddhist belief, is when a person reaches the point where he or she loses all desire for worldly things. Such persons are then ready to pass into a place of eternal bliss called *nirvana*.

Anyone who follows the rules of the religion may become *a* Buddha, or Enlightened One. However, when Buddhists speak of *the* Buddha, they mean one man—Prince Siddhartha Gautama, an Indian prince who lived from about 563 B.C. to 483 B.C. His name, Siddhartha, means "one whose aim is accomplished." He is also known as *Sakyamuni*, or "Sage of the Sakya Tribe." Buddhists sometimes call him *Bhagavan*, or "the Blessed One."

Today, Buddhism is one of the world's great religions. It has more than 249 million followers. Most of these are in Asia. The countries with the largest Buddhist populations are Sri Lanka (formerly Ceylon), China, Tibet, Mongolia, Laos, Vietnam, Thailand, Korea, and Japan. Although Buddhism was born in India, it almost died out there and has only started to revive in recent years.

THE BUDDHA'S EARLY LIFE

Prince Siddhartha's father was ruler of a small state in northern India. When the child was born, his father sent for fortune tellers. They predicted that the boy would someday leave his home and family. This would happen, they said, when the prince learned about sorrow, sickness, and death.

This greatly disturbed the king, for Prince Siddhartha was heir to the throne. He gave orders that all knowledge of sorrow, sickness, and death should be kept from the prince. A special palace was built for Siddhartha. According to the *Buddhacarita* ("Acts of the Buddha"), written by the poet Ashvaghosha, the prince lived in the upper stories in rooms as beautiful as if they had come from heaven. Siddhartha didn't want to leave the palace since all his desires were satisfied there. In time, he was married to a beautiful princess and had a son named Rahula.

THE FOUR MEN

The years passed and Prince Siddhartha continued to live in a protected and pampered way. Then one day he heard the palace dancing girls talking about how beautiful the trees were in the groves beyond the palace. The prince had never seen trees, for he had never left the palace in his life.

He asked his father for permission to visit the groves. The king agreed, but only after he sent soldiers to drive away any person who suggested sorrow, sickness, or death. However, the prince did happen to see one old man. He was astonished, for he had never seen a very old person before. He asked his charioteer what this meant and the man explained the meaning of old age and how it affects a person. The prince was deeply disturbed. According to Ashvaghosha's account, the prince said sadly:

"So this is how old age destroys the memory, the beauty, the strength of us all! And yet the world does not seem to care. Return to the palace. How can I take delight in the park when my heart is disturbed by fear of growing old!"

Later, he took another trip. This time he saw a sick man and was as deeply affected as he had been by the sorrowful old man. On still another trip he saw a corpse.

Siddhartha returned to the palace more disturbed than ever. He lost all interest in his former life of pleasure. He thought only of sorrow, sickness, and death. He felt that something could be done about these miseries of the earth, but he did not know what.

Then one day, while roaming in the woods alone, he met a fourth man. This man was a ragged religious beggar. The prince questioned the man, who told him:

"I am terrified by birth and death. I have adopted a homeless life. I have no possessions or hope of any. Since all the world is sorrow, sickness, and death, I seek that blessed state where there are none of these. I wander about, intent upon this supreme goal, accepting such alms as people give me."

THE BUDDHA'S SEARCH

Prince Siddhartha—the future Buddha—realized then that this ragged beggar expressed his own thoughts. He also wanted to find the state where sorrow, sickness, and death were extinct. He knew that he could not find any answers while remaining in his father's palace of pleasure. He decided to leave his home and family, seeking enlightenment in a religious life as the old beggar was doing.

His father objected, but the prince pointed out that he left behind a son who could take his place as the king's heir. The king sorrowfully gave his consent. Siddhartha then left his home, taking with him only the robe he wore, the sandals on his feet, and a bowl for the food he would beg for the rest of his life. He was then twenty-nine years old.

The future Buddha at first sought his answers in the Hindu religion, studying under its *gurus* ("teachers"). Hinduism had been brought to India by the Aryans, a people from central Asia who had invaded India about 1500 B.C. The Aryans had driven back the darkskinned Dravidian Indians and became the ruling class.

The Aryans had worshiped many gods, the chief of whom was the war god Indra. By the time Prince Siddhartha began to study Hinduism, Indra had faded into the background. His place as chief of the gods was taken by a trinity (three gods working together). These three were Brahma, the Creator of Life; Vishnu, the Preserver of Life; and Siva, the Destroyer of Life.

In addition to these three leaders, Hinduism has thousands of other gods. Most of these are *avatars*. An avatar is one of the trinity (Brahma, Vishnu, or Siva) who permits himself to be born again in a human body. The god does this to return to earth and help people.

In accepting the Hindu religious life, Prince Siddhartha could

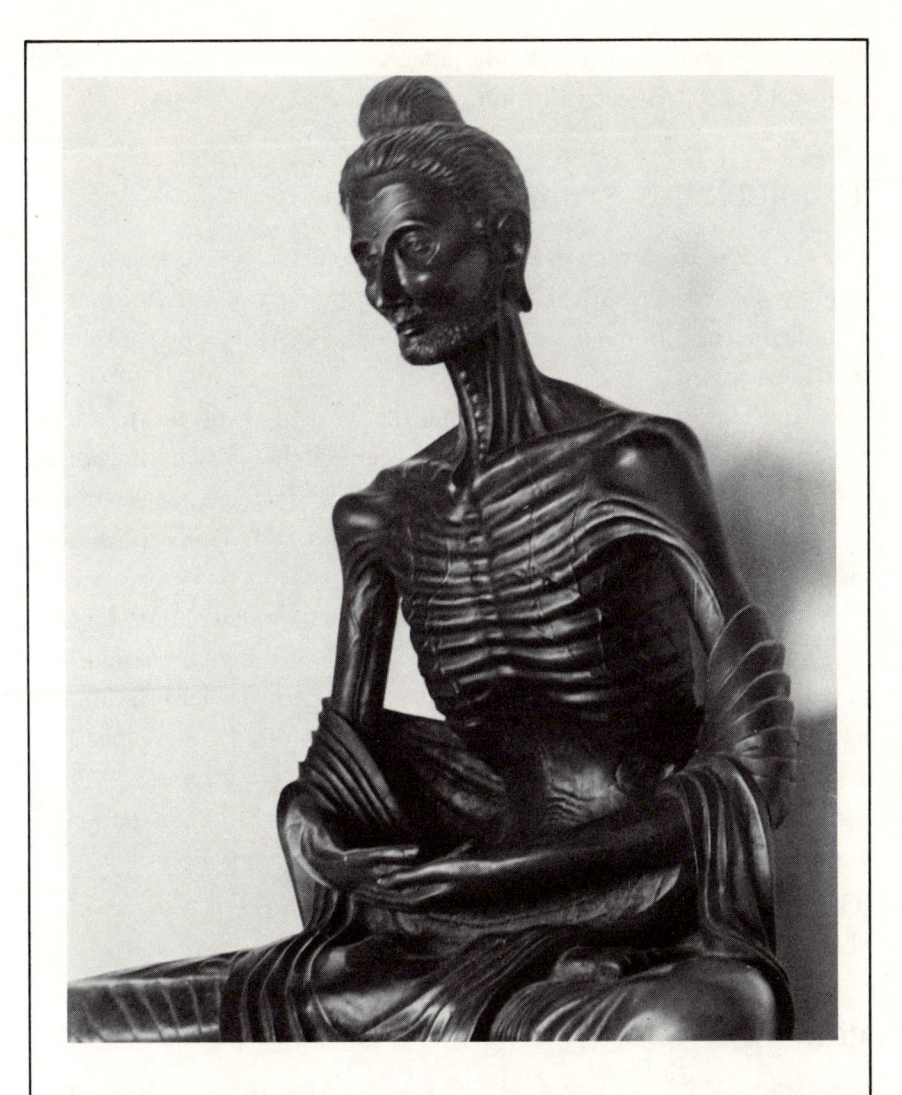

An Indian statue shows the Buddha in his Hindu period fasting until he was reduced to skin and bones.

choose any god or avatar as his personal god. He also learned that the world is unreal—an illusion.

THE BUDDHA'S STUDIES

For six years the future Buddha moved from teacher to teacher. He quickly absorbed what each had to teach, but was never satisfied by what he learned. Some teachings he agreed with. Others he considered totally wrong.

The Hindu religion teaches that the world is a place of misery. Prince Siddhartha agreed. He also accepted the Hindu concept of *reincarnation,* or rebirth. According to this doctrine, each time a person dies, he or she is reborn to live another life. This rebirth goes on and on.

The number of times one must be reborn depends upon *karma.* One's karma is the sum of all the good and bad things a person does in a lifetime. If a person has a good karma, it is because he or she has done more good deeds than bad. The gurus taught the prince that a beggar may be reborn as a king if he has a good karma. A king with a bad karma may be reborn a slave, an animal, a homeless ghost, or even as an insect. Each future life depends upon one's actions in the previous life. Hindu writers describe this endless cycle of rebirths as the Wheel of Life.

MOKSHA

It is bad karma that keeps a Hindu bound to the Wheel of Life. The object of the Hindu religion is to help a person escape from the recycle of births. This can be done by overcoming karma. Then, instead of returning to the misery of earth, the Hindu enters *moksha.*

Moksha is the Hindu version of heaven. When a person ceases to be reborn and goes back into the body of Brahma, the Creator of Life, he or she enters moksha. Every person is a small part of Brahma and returns to the source.

When entering moksha, a person is in a state of eternal happiness and bliss, completely freed from the miseries of the earth. This was what Siddhartha sought, but he did not find it. Finally, he turned to the *ascetic* teachers, who taught him that moksha could only be achieved by fasting and punishing the flesh in order to free the spirit.

For a time, Siddhartha followed the teachings of the ascetics with total dedication. Still he did not achieve moksha. In later talks with his monks, the Buddha told about the miseries of this period of his life:

"Naked was I, flouting all decency. I took first only one morsel of food a day. Then I took one morsel every two days. Then only one every seven days. I pulled out the hair of my head and the hair of my beard. I crouched on thorns. I lived in torment, so great were the lengths I went in asceticism."

He found that self-torture was hurting rather than helping him achieve moksha. His mind became dull from starvation and suffering. He decided then that the Hindu way to salvation was wrong. He had studied its teaching intensely, and nothing had happened. He decided that he must seek the way to salvation within his own mind.

MEDITATION

The future Buddha knew that salvation could come only from within himself. He could expect help from no one. He started to eat again. Five ascetics who had been studying with him now left. They could not believe there was any way to moksha except through self-denial and bodily torture. They said that Siddhartha had failed.

Siddhartha now turned to *meditation*—deep, personal religious thought so intense that it was as tiring as heavy labor. Proper meditation is extremely difficult to do. It requires great powers of concentration. Buddhists practice for a long time before they can meditate properly. All thoughts must be removed from the conscious mind except the point being meditated upon.

In this manner the future Buddha sought to find the secret of salvation.

MARA THE TEMPTER

One day while sitting under a fig tree, Siddhartha went into such deep meditation that he concentrated all night. The earliest account of this tells us that in the first part of the night, he began to remember his past lives on earth. Later, he acquired the ability to read the lives of others. In the final part of the night, he understood the Four Noble Truths, which are the basic laws of Buddhism. When this knowledge came to him, Siddhartha became enlightened. From that moment on he was the Buddha, or Enlightened One.

A different story is told in later Buddhist scriptures. In these accounts Mara the Tempter, an evil spirit, saw the future Buddha meditating under the fig tree. Mara realized that the prince was near enlightenment. He called his three daughters—Desire, Discontent, and Passion—and his evil servants to help him stop the future Buddha from discovering the secret of enlightenment.

Mara and his helpers attacked the prince with storms, a rain of hot rocks, sandstorms, and showers of mud. All these lost their power before they reached the meditating man. The evil enemy then attacked with swords, spears, and arrows, but the weapons turned to flowers and fell at Siddhartha's feet. Finally, after many trials, the tempter gave up and withdrew. Siddhartha continued his meditation and, in the last part of the night, understood the Four Noble Truths, gaining enlightenment. He was thirty-five years old and had been seeking this goal for six years.

THE BELIEFS OF THE BUDDHA

The Buddha based his beliefs upon Hinduism, but made changes to fit his own ideas and experiences. He accepted nothing until assured that it worked for him. In this way he developed practical beliefs that he felt could be followed by all people.

The Buddha accepted the Hindu idea of rebirth and the Wheel of Life. He believed in karma and that it was the cause of people being reborn into this world of misery. However, he did not believe in moksha or in the Hindu belief that moksha is a mystical union of the freed soul with Brahma. He rejected this because he did not believe in any god or gods or in a human soul. He said that nothing could join with Brahma because there was no Brahma.

However, the Buddha believed in something similar to moksha. He called it nirvana. The Buddha never explained what nirvana is. It takes the place of heaven in other religions, but is not like the ordinary idea of heaven.

THE NATURE OF NIRVANA

Some scholars believe that nirvana is not a real place at all. They say it is only a state of mind that one reaches through meditation.

Those who believe that nirvana is real admit that it appears to be a place where one does nothing but meditate.

While the Buddha refused to explain the nature of nirvana, his followers often attempted to do so. In *The Questions of King Milinda,* a famous Buddhist text, the teacher Nagasena explains nirvana to the questioning king:

> *As the lotus flower is unstained by water, so is nirvana unstained. As water slacks the heat of fever, so does nirvana slack the heat of passions and removes the craving for earthly enjoyments. As medicine protects the body from poisons, so does nirvana protect from passion's poisons. As medicine cures sickness, so does nirvana put an end to suffering. Nirvana shares with space the qualities that neither are born, grow old, nor are reborn. Like the wishing jewel, nirvana grants all one can desire of joy and bliss. Nirvana is as lofty as a mountain peak and unshakable.*

The king replied, "So be it, Nagasena. As such I accept it."

BUDDHA AND THE SOUL

The Hindus call the soul *atman.* The Buddha did not agree that this soul returns to Brahma when it escapes the Wheel of Life. The Buddha did not believe in either Brahma or the soul. However, he knew there had to be something eternal in human beings or they could not be born again.

The Buddha said that this eternal part is a person's karma. In the Hindu belief, karma is the sum of one's good and bad deeds. The Buddha accepted this. The Hindu also believes that karma determines the kind of life one will have after being born again. The

Buddha accepted this also. However, he went further and gave karma the place that other religions give the human soul.

How does karma survive after death?

The Buddha explained that a person's body is made of earth, water, fire, and wind. To these are added our various senses and the knowledge we gain in our life. In addition, there is karma.

Karma is all that remains when we die and our bodies decay. It then acts as a magnet to draw more earth, water, fire, and wind to create a new body for the next rebirth.

REBIRTH AND THE RIVER

If everything about us is lost after death except the result of our past deeds (karma), does our new body really contain the same person who died?

A Buddhist is likely to answer the question like this:

"Watch a flowing river. Observe the water flowing between the river's banks. Go tomorrow and look at the same river again. It *is* the same river. It has the same shape, the same banks, and the same tree and grasses grow along its banks. But the *water* flowing between these banks is not the same water that we saw yesterday. The stream and the water may look the same, but the water of yesterday has already flowed down to the sea. This is new water, but can we honestly say that the river itself has changed?"

THE FIRST SERMON

After finding enlightenment under the fig tree, the Buddha faced a fateful decision. He could enter nirvana for an eternity of happiness and bliss. Or he could choose to remain on earth to help others find the path to salvation.

The Buddha believed that he had discovered new ideas in the search for salvation. If he did not remain on earth, there would be no one to teach them.

After making his decision to remain on earth, the Buddha went to Banaras. Here in this holy city of the Hindu religion, he met the five men who had deserted him when he gave up the ascetic life. Soon they became his disciples.

The Buddha preached his first sermon in a deer park near Banaras. In this sermon the Buddha revealed the Four Noble Truths which form the basis of Buddhist beliefs. He also revealed the Eightfold Path. This is a list of the things a Buddhist must do to stop desire and craving for worldly things.

The Buddha's Four Noble Truths are:

1. All lives, from birth to death, are filled with suffering.
2. This suffering is caused by a craving for worldly things.
3. Suffering will stop when one learns to suppress desire.
4. We can learn to suppress desire by following the Eightfold Path.

THE EIGHTFOLD PATH

The Eightfold Path revealed by the Buddha in his sermon in the deer park are eight things a person must do to overcome craving for earthly pleasures and thus destroy karma. They are:

1. *The Right View.* Understanding of the Buddha's Four Noble Truths.
2. *The Right Thought.* Having friendly thoughts about people and all other forms of life.
3. *The Right Speech.* Speaking kindly and truthfully while avoiding bitter words against anyone or anything.

A Japanese Buddhist priest makes his early morning devotional prayer.

4. *The Right Action.* Acting skillfully and with sympathy while avoiding vain or violent effort.
5. *The Right Work.* Earning a living in a way that will not harm another.
6. *The Right Effort.* Using one's time for self-improvement.
7. *The Right Mindfulness.* Keeping the right state of mind—self-awareness and compassion. Only then can a person's mind control his thoughts and his body's actions.
8. *The Right Concentration.* Removing other concerns from one's mind in order to concentrate properly on religious meditation. The intense Buddhist meditation, focused to a single point, leads to an awakening of the mind. This can lead to enlightenment and to nirvana.

THE BROTHERHOOD

After his first sermon, the Buddha moved from town to town, preaching. In a short time his followers increased to sixty. They formed a *sangha,* or community of monks.

Here again, the Buddha broke with Hindu tradition. The Hindus were bound by the caste system which divided society into four groups. The first and highest was the priestly caste. The second and ruling caste was the warrior class. The merchant class made up the third caste, and laborers made up the lowest caste. Below the four castes were the untouchables, or outcastes. A person was born into a caste according to his or her karma and could not rise above this station in one lifetime.

Buddha believed in karma, but disagreed with the segregation of the caste system. He welcomed every caste into his sangha. In his view every person was entitled to work toward salvation. However, he did not accept everyone into the sangha who applied. Murderers, thieves, slaves, rapists, adulterers, troublemakers, and people without hands and feet could not join.

Criminals and troublemakers, of course, were excluded because their actions violate the loving nature of Buddhism. It is more difficult to understand a religion barring the crippled. There does not seem to be a reason given in Buddhist scriptures. It appears to have been for practical purposes. The monks in the beginning did not have permanent homes. They moved from place to place, only settling down during the rainy season when travel was difficult. A person without feet or legs could not travel easily. In a like manner, one without hands could not properly care for himself.

WOMEN IN THE SANGHA

In the early days the Buddha only admitted men into the sangha. Ananda, a favorite follower of the Buddha, begged the Blessed One to permit women to join. Later, the Buddha's stepmother asked him to accept women. Again he refused. He was afraid that the presence of women would disrupt the monks' thoughts.

Then, close to the end of the Buddha's life, Ananda tried again.

"Can women reach nirvana?" he asked.

The Buddha replied that they could. "Then why can they not join the sangha?" Ananda asked. "You formed the sangha to help others find the road to salvation. Who will help the women?"

The Buddha then agreed to permit Buddhist nuns. He did not like to do so. He said that without women the sangha would last a thousand years. It would last only five hundred years if women members were permitted.

In permitting women to join the sangha, the Buddha made it

plain that they occupied a position below men. Nuns were required to show respect to monks. A monk could criticize a nun, but a nun could not criticize a monk.

While a number of stories are told of various nuns, women never played a large role in the sangha and were not encouraged to join. This was especially true if they were young and beautiful. There is a touching story told of the Japanese nun Ryonen. She was handmaiden to the empress. When her mistress died, Ryonen realized that life is an unhappy state. She decided to live a religious life. Every monastery she applied to refused to take her because she was too beautiful. They feared the effect of her beauty upon the monks. After the last refusal, she built a fire, heated a piece of iron, and placed it against her face. Now scarred and ugly, she reapplied for membership. She was accepted.

THE PRECEPTS

Candidates to join the sangha had to be at least fifteen years old. Each had to appear before ten older monks and make three statements:

"I take refuge in the Buddha."

"I take refuge in the dharma." (*Dharma* is Buddhist spiritual law. It is based upon the teachings of the Buddha.)

"I take refuge in the sangha."

The novices then shaved their heads and exchanged their clothes for yellow robes. They began their religious education by learning the "Precepts."

The Precepts are rules of conduct. Some of them are very much like the Ten Commandments of the Bible. The first five of these religious laws apply to all Buddhists. They are:

1. Kill no living thing. (This even includes insects.)

2. Do not steal or cheat.
3. Always be chaste.
4. Tell no lies.
5. Drink no intoxicants. Take no drugs.

Other Precepts apply only to monks and nuns. Some of them are:

6. Eat only at the appointed time.
7. Avoid anything that excites the senses.
8. Do not wear adornments. (This includes perfume.)
9. Avoid handling money or touching gold.
10. Do not speak ill of anyone.
11. Do not show anger.
12. Abide by that which is right.

These laws, which were created by the first sangha, are still in force today. The number of Precepts varies with different sects. There are 227 in use in Thailand, for example. Chinese Buddhists observe 250, and Tibetan Buddhists have 253.

LIFE IN THE SANGHA

In the beginning the monks traveled from place to place, learning from the Buddha and later teaching themselves. Present-day monasteries had their beginnings in the little huts and shelters the monks put up for themselves during the three-month rainy season. Later, rich laymen came to believe that they would gain merit—thus helping their own karma—by providing places for the monks to stay.

The sangha was a democratic organization. The monks governed themselves. As the order grew in number, committees were formed to decide questions in the same manner that people send rep-

The beautiful Buddhist temples seen today had their beginnings in the huts devout people donated to the Buddha's monks.

Left: the statues in this temple are not for worship. They are reminders of the goodness of the Buddha. This shows a temple abbot in Bangkok. Right: in rural areas of Cambodia traditional Buddhist monks conduct schools.

resentatives to their governments. The Buddha remained the final authority. When the committees could not decide a question, it was taken to him. His decisions and teachings then became the dharma, or spiritual law, of Buddhism.

Every two weeks there was an assembly for all monks, and the Precepts were read. There was a pause after each to permit any monk or nun who had violated the law to arise and confess. Punishment depended upon the offense. The four great crimes were misconduct with the opposite sex, theft, murder, and claiming magic powers. These were punished by expulsion from the order.

Buddhist monks and nuns did not work. They lived on charity. Their time was spent in studying, meditating, and sometimes teaching those who gave them food and shelter. They listened to the sermons of the Buddha and constantly asked him questions.

THE MIDDLE WAY

The Buddha often talked of his rich life before he abandoned his home. Then he would tell of the agonies he went through in trying to follow the ways of the Hindu ascetics. In one of his sermons to the monks, he said:

Both those foolish ones who torment themselves and those who surrender to delight of the senses are deluded. Austerities confuse the mind because the body is exhausted. Those who practice such self-punishment can understand neither the ordinary things of life or the Right Path to Truth which lies beyond the senses. Likewise, the mind of those who let themselves be overwhelmed by passion and worldly delusion are still less able to see the way to Truth. So I gave up both extreme ways. I sought and found a better Path—the Middle Way which goes between these two.

The Buddha then explained that his Middle Way consisted in understanding the Four Noble Truths and following the Eightfold Path.

DEVELOPMENT OF THE DHARMA

The dharma, or spiritual law, developed from these sermons and from the questions the Buddha's followers asked. It was further refined by the *sutras*, spiritual narratives of the Buddha, written by others. These writings became the Pali canon, the oldest Buddhist text. Pali is a literary language used only by Buddhists. Later Buddhist writings were in Sanskrit, the common Hindu dialect.

In his sermons and discussions with his monks, the Buddha answered most questions freely. However, he refused to explain nirvana. The monks had a great interest in this, as do modern Buddhists. Once, a monk became angry after repeatedly asking the Buddha for an explanation of the true state of nirvana. He said that if the Buddha did not know, he should say so.

The Buddha replied that people were suffering from the misery of life and rebirths. People needed immediate help. He then told the story of a man who had been wounded by an arrow. Friends called a doctor, but the wounded man refused to let the doctor touch him until he answered some questions. The man wanted to know the caste of the archer who had shot him. He asked the length of the arrow and what kind it was. And so on through many questions.

"You," the Buddha said to his questioner, "are like this injured man. You waste time in useless questions. Instead, spend your time seeking ways to end your suffering. Then you will find out what nirvana is. No one will have to tell you."

This story illustrates a point the Buddha continually made to his followers—that no one can show anyone else the road to salvation. Sermons, teachers, and dharma can show one how to act, but salvation itself is a personal thing that must be learned through difficult and intense meditation.

THE JATAKA TALES

One of the fruits of the Buddha's enlightenment was the ability to recall all of his former lives, or incarnations. There were thousands of them. In time about five hundred were collected into what became known as the Jataka (or "Rebirth") Tales of the Buddha. These stories, which point out Buddhist morals or beliefs, often resemble the Indian *Ocean of Stories* fables and the fables of Aesop.

One of the Jataka Tales tells about the Buddha stopping to smell a pretty flower. A fairy appeared and reproved the Blessed One.

"You are guilty of theft," the fairy complained. "The perfume of the flower was not yours. You stole it by not asking permission."

Theft is one of the gravest sins of Buddhism, for a Buddhist monk renounces property. This Jataka tale points out to us that there is no such thing as a "small" theft. The theft of even the perfume of a flower violates the spirit of Buddhism.

THE LION'S SKIN

In another famous Jataka tale, the Buddha used a story of a past life to point out the value of keeping one's mouth shut. This came about after a monk said more than the Buddha thought he should have.

In this story the future Buddha was living as a farmer. A ped-

An example of the Ajanta cave paintings that illustrated the "Jataka Tales." These paintings, in Maharashtra, India, were made over a period from the second century B.C. to about the seventh century A.D.

dler, to avoid buying grain for the ass that carried his wares, dressed the little animal in a lion's skin. He then turned the ass loose in various farmers' barley fields. The farmers, thinking it was a lion, were afraid to drive it away. Then the ass happened to bray and the future Buddha realized that it was no lion. Angry farmers came and tore away the lion's skin, beating the beast unmercifully.

The Buddha concluded the story by saying that he had been the wise farmer in this past life. Kokalika (the talkative monk) had been the ass who was not smart enough to know when to keep his mouth shut.

THE MUSTARD SEED

One of the best known of the Jataka Tales is the famous story of the mustard seed. In it the Buddha meets an old woman who is bewailing the misery of her life. She asks the Buddha for his help. He explains that all life is suffering. The only way to escape is to overcome karma and enter nirvana.

She will not listen to this argument. So he tells her to bring him a mustard seed from a house that has never known sorrow and trouble. He will use the seed to banish all her miseries. The old woman was delighted. She set out to find such a house and the Buddha continued on his way. Much later he returned to the same place.

He found the old woman singing to herself as she washed clothes by the riverside. He had already seen with his spiritual eye what had happened to her. But he asked anyway if she had found the house with no unhappiness.

"No, Blessed One," she replied. "Every house I visited had far more troubles than I have."

"Are you still seeking?" the Buddha asked.

"Later I will," the old woman replied. "Right now I must stop and help these people, for they are less fortunate than I."

"Then you do not need the mustard seed," the Blessed One replied. "You are on the road to becoming a Buddha yourself."

This story illustrates the Buddhist belief that helping others is one of the greatest of virtues. It helps build a good karma and—as the story points out—puts one on the road to becoming a Buddha also.

DEATH OF THE BUDDHA

The Buddha continued to preach until he was eighty years old. He became gravely ill after eating a meal. Some accounts say it was tainted pork. It became clear to his followers that he would soon die. Ananda, who had been with the Buddha for twenty years, tearfully asked who would lead them after the Buddha's death. He had often asked the Blessed One to name a successor. In the past the Buddha had always refused. Now as he approached death, the Buddha again refused.

"Be lamps unto yourselves," he said. This was in keeping with his belief that every person must save himself.

As he lay dying, the Buddha told his disciples that he had done all he could do both for himself and for others. Therefore there was no reason for him to remain on earth. "Monks, hereafter my dharma shall guide generation after generation of people. . . . When the light of spiritual law has dispelled the darkness of life, when all existence has been proven an illusion, peace will come at last to cure life's long sickness. The time for my entry into nirvana has come. I have spoken my last words."

THE SPREAD OF BUDDHISM

Buddhism was a simple and democratic religion that could appeal to ordinary people. Even so, the religion spread slowly during the first two hundred years after Sakyamuni's death. In the early years most Buddhists lived in the Ganges River plains area.

Things began to change after Emperor Asoka of the Indian Mauryan empire became a Buddhist.

Asoka, who lived from about 273 B.C. to 232 B.C., is second only to Buddha Sakyamuni in importance in early days of Buddhism. He was a Hindu king who waged bloody wars to unite India into a single nation. After much fighting, only Kalinga, a small state, remained independent. Asoka attacked it, but the Kalingans fought so bravely that over a hundred thousand soldiers were killed. Asoka was so shocked that he became a Buddhist. He swore that he would never again lead an army into war. He devoted the rest of his life to the spread of Buddhism.

THE KING'S MISSIONARIES

Asoka sent Buddhist missionaries to Egypt, Syria, Macedonia, China, and other far places.

In Ceylon (present Sri Lanka) the missionaries converted the royal family. Then the religion spread through the kingdom, replacing Hinduism and animism (the worship of natural spirits).

The spread of Buddhism to Ceylon was extremely fortunate for the religion. Missionaries to the other countries were not immediately successful. Then, when Buddhism died out in India, it was kept alive in Ceylon until it could gain a foothold in China, Southeast Asia, and Japan.

After Asoka died, later Indian kings did not support Buddhism. They thought the religion removed too many people from the work force. Buddha's message of peace also conflicted with the warlike natures of these kings. Another reason for the gradual decline of Buddhism was the rise of Sivaism. This was a new Hindu cult built around the god Siva. It was less strict than Buddhism, and it promised more to the common people. Anyone could take part. Under the Buddha's teachings only a person who abandoned the world and devoted himself or herself entirely to religious activity could hope for salvation.

Another blow to Buddhism came in the seventh century A.D. when Muhammad founded the Islamic religion in Arabia. Islam was a very militant religion. Its followers conquered Afghanistan in A.D. 644 and took over the Buddhist state of Sind (now southern Pakistan) in A.D. 710. During the next three centuries there was a gradual takeover of India. The conquerors hated the Hindu religion and considered Buddhism just another Hindu sect. The persecution caused many to convert to Islam.

BUDDHISM MOVES EAST

Asoka's original missionaries were not successful except in Ceylon. Then, gradually, the faith began to take hold outside of India and

Angkor Wat was built in the twelfth century. This great Buddhist temple is one of the wonders of the world.

Ceylon. It became popular in China about A.D. 100. Then two hundred years later Korea absorbed Buddhism from China. Korean missionaries then introduced the belief to Japan in A.D. 551. In the same year, Indians carried it to Burma, and in A.D. 600, Buddhism reached Tibet. From Burma the religion spread to Thailand.

Buddhism also spread through Indonesia where the Saliendra kings of Java built the magnificent Borobudur temple. The religion was then introduced into Cambodia in A.D. 997 by King Suryavarman I, ruler of a Malay state. The king, who had a Cambodian mother, invaded Cambodia and substituted Buddhism for the Hindu religion he found there. In Cambodia, Buddhism resulted in the building of Angkor Wat, a great temple that is considered one of the wonders of the modern world.

Later, Buddhism died out in Indonesia and Malaya, being replaced by Islam, the Muslim religion. In the other countries it has continued to this day.

THE TWO BUDDHISMS

Changes began to creep into Buddhism within the first hundred years after the Buddha's death. These changes eventually split the religion into two main divisions. No one knows exactly when this split occurred. But it came about because not enough people could follow the religion as the Buddha established it. Not everyone could abandon home and employment to seek life in a religious community.

The first of the divisions is Theravada Buddhism. (*Theravada* means "Doctrine of the Elders.") Its followers say it continues the original teachings of the Buddha. The second division is Mahayana Buddhism. (*Mahayana* means "the Great Vehicle.") It is so called because its followers say that it can carry more people to salvation than Theravada Buddhism can.

THERAVADA BUDDHISM

Theravada Buddhism for centuries was called Hinayana, a word that means "the Little Vehicle." It was given this name by Mahayana Buddhists as a term of contempt because only a few people—the

A crowded devotional service in Thailand at which children are also present.

monks—could ride it to salvation. In 1950, at the World Fellowship of Buddhists meeting in Colombo, Sri Lanka, Hinayana Buddhists adopted the name Theravada. It was selected to show that this was the oldest of the Buddhist organizations.

Theravada Buddhism is a personal religion. That is, salvation is something that each person must accomplish himself or herself. Teachers can only point the way and help us to understand laws and concepts.

MAHAYANA BUDDHISM

Theravada Buddhism teaches that the Buddha was a man—a superman, perhaps, but still a man. Mahayana Buddhists have an entirely different view of the Blessed One. They have raised the Buddha to the rank of a god.

Mahayana Buddhists believe that there are many Buddhas, although there is only one who can be called *the* Buddha. These other Buddhas are saints who can aid humanity in finding salvation. One of the sutras in the Mahayana canon tells us that the number of such Buddhas is greater than the number of grains of sand along the banks of the mighty Ganges River in India.

These other Buddhas are called *bodhisattvas*. They are people who have achieved enlightenment. But like the Buddha, they delayed entering nirvana because of their great love for humanity. They have remained to help others find the road to salvation.

A bodhisattva may walk the earth as the Buddha did. Or the bodhisattva may live in a Buddhist heaven. He or she can answer prayer.

Each bodhisattva personifies a trait of the Buddha. For example, the bodhisattva Manjusri is the Buddha's wisdom. The Buddha's

Two bodhisattvas. *Left: a Chinese eighth-century wooden figure. Right: a Gandhara stone statue shows a mixture of Greek and Indian influences.*

pity and sympathy for humankind is personified in the popular bodhisattva *Avalokitesvara* (pronounced uv-ā-*low*'-key-tash-ver-ā). The name means "the Lord who looks down."

This bodhisattva is often pictured as having many eyes or faces. This is so that he can look in all directions to seek for suffering humanity. The famous Bayon towers of Angkor Thom, an ancient Cambodian city, have over two hundred faces of this bodhisattva carved on them.

MAHAYANA–THERAVADA DIFFERENCES

The Buddha believed that each person must find his or her own way to salvation. Yet the Mahayana belief is that bodhisattvas have the ability to help ordinary people to salvation. This appears contrary to the Buddha's teachings.

However, when one questions Mahayana Buddhists on these points, the answer is that this is not contrary to the Buddha's teachings at all. Then we are told the story of the time the Blessed One showed a handful of leaves to his followers.

"Are there more leaves in my hand than there are in the trees of the forest?" he asked them.

The disciples replied that the leaves in his hand were few. Those of the woods were countless in number.

"In the same manner," the Buddha replied, "the things I have told you are like the leaves in my hand. They are few in number. Much more are those things I have not told you. They are as many as the leaves of the forest."

Thus many of the differences between Theravada and Mahayana Buddhism are due to Mahayana developing those things which the Buddha did not tell about.

Buddha gave authority for changes. He told his monks that he had given them the Truth and the Discipline through his teaching and the examples of his life. The Four Noble Truths and the major Precepts could not be changed, but lesser Precepts could be.

Theravada and Mahayana Buddhism emphasize different parts of the Buddha's life and messages. The Theravadan Buddhists say that the important part of the Buddha's teachings is the search for salvation. Nirvana is the all-important goal. Only those things that help us toward nirvana are important. However, this does not mean that we should be selfish in our pursuit of salvation. Love and sympathy for others build good karma which aids in breaking the chain of rebirths that keeps us from becoming enlightened.

Mahayana Buddhism emphasizes the part of the Buddha's life after his enlightenment. When he became enlightened, he reached the goal sought by Theravada Buddhists. He could have entered nirvana and forgotten the world, but instead, he chose to endure the world's misery for another forty-five years. Mahayana Buddhists say that this proves the Buddha was more concerned with helping others than with his own personal salvation.

"If we only guide our lives by the words of the Buddha as they have come down to us in the sutras," a Buddhist teacher said, "then we miss half of the Blessed One's teachings. These other teachings are in his actions—in the things he did to help others."

All of the various religious sects have been created by exactly these kinds of differences. Each takes as important something that the other feels is less important.

THE NATURE OF CREATION

The Mahayana *Lotus of the Good Law* sutra says the Buddha is a god who is father of the world. He has lived for countless ages, and will continue to live forever. He first gained enlightenment untold *kalpas* ago.

A kalpa is a measurement of time that extends from the beginning of a world to the end of that world. The Buddha explained the meaning of a kalpa like this: Imagine a mountain as large as any the world has ever known. Once each thousand years a man takes a soft rag and wipes one gentle stroke across the face of this giant mountain. The friction of his soft rag will wear away the mountain before one single kalpa has passed.

In another sutra the Buddha tells about the earth's beginnings. Originally the world was in darkness. There was only water. Then land began to form on the water. The only living creatures were beings made of light. These creatures were reborn from a world that died at the end of the previous kalpa. These luminous creatures began to eat things of this new earth. They found the taste pleasant. This started them craving earthly things and pleasures, as a dope addict craves narcotics. They then lost their spiritual bodies and became as men are today. This made them subject to sorrow, sickness, and death.

The fall of these spiritual creatures marks the end of the first period of a kalpa. Up to this point the story bears a striking resemblance to the biblical book of Genesis. In Genesis we read that "darkness was upon the face of the deep." Then God made light and finally Adam and Eve, who were originally spiritual creatures. Like the luminous creatures of Mahayana Buddhism, they ate of the Tree of Knowledge and fell from grace.

The second period of a kalpa is like our present historical period where the people live in sorrow, sickness, and finally death. It is a period of misery and suffering. In the third period of a single kalpa, the world begins to dissolve. In the fourth period, the world is destroyed and the kalpa has ended. A new kalpa immediately starts with luminous creatures who survived the end of the previous world. Kalpas follow kalpas like the waves of an ocean. So time continues forever. Worlds continue to be born and die.

THE BUDDHA ILLUSIONS

In the *Lotus* sutra the Buddha revealed that he gained enlightenment many kalpas ago. Since that time he has been reborn into the world countless times. He did this to bring the Buddhist law to humankind.

None of the Buddhas born during these many kalpas was real. Each was an illusion created by the mind of the real Buddha—the god Buddha. In each rebirth the illusionary Buddha lived as a man. He went through the motions of seeking enlightenment, although he had been enlightened many kalpas ago. He did this to *show* the people the way to salvation. By observing the life of the Buddha, men and women could see one like themselves escape from the sorrows of the Wheel of Life.

In coming to earth in a body of flesh to save humankind, the Buddha can be compared to the later Jesus Christ. In fact, there is an old Mahayana story of an aged monk who heard for the first time the story of Jesus. "That man," he said of Christ, "is almost a Buddha." In his opinion, he could pay no higher compliment.

While there is a comparison between the way each was born to save humankind, there is also a major difference which is important to each religion. Christ was born only once, and His death on the cross provided the way to salvation for all time. The Buddha continues to be born through all time.

OTHER BUDDHIST SCHOOLS ❧

Mahayana Buddhism is based upon the great love the Buddha and the bodhisattvas have for all living things. One of the Jataka Tales recounts a story about the extreme lengths to which the Buddha once went in expressing this love:

In one of his former lives the Blessed One found a hungry tigress in the woods. She was so weak from lack of food and drink that she could not move. Seven tiny cubs, also starving, crouched beside her. The Buddha was so touched by pity and so filled with love for living things that he sacrificed his life to the tigress that she and her cubs might live.

The Buddha's love developed into the idea of the bodhisattva, who lives to help others. This loving ideal, in turn, gave rise to new schools of Buddhist thought which accepted the idea of salvation through prayer.

JAPANESE PURE LAND

The Pure Land school was introduced into Japan in the thirteenth century. It became very popular and is still so today. Salvation comes from repeating the words, *Namu Amida Butsu*, which mean, "Homage to the Buddha Amida."

Pure Land Buddhism saves through love, prayer, and faith. The Buddha Amida (Amitabha) has sometimes been compared to Jehovah of the Judeo-Christian religions. Buddhists say that Jehovah is a God of love and justice. He makes the religious laws and then judges and punishes the sinners. Amitabha, on the other hand, is only love. He rewards, but does not punish. A sinner, in his view, punishes himself.

THE PURE LAND HEAVEN

The heaven of Pure Land Buddhism is a place of surpassing beauty. A Sanskrit manuscript, *Description of the Happy Land,* tells what this paradise is like. The trees are covered with flowers that glow like lamps, gold and jewels abound, birds of great beauty flutter about. And there are lovely girls to charm the faithful.

The *Description* says that the girls, who never grow old, are there to "captivate with their playfulness the wearied minds of the ascetics."

The presence of young girls is a radical departure from the usual Buddhist prohibitions on the association of monks and nuns with the opposite sex.

The *Description* says: "Those who have done deeds of merit live happily. They do in the Heaven of the West as they desire. Life for them is always joyful. Each shines with his own light. Each lives in a station determined by his past deeds."

Chinese Buddhists at a temple in Taipei, Taiwan, pray to Amitabha Buddha.

MAGIC BUDDHISM

There are so many Buddhist sects that it is impossible to discuss them all. However, two should be mentioned because of their unusualness. One is *Tantrism*, the "magic Buddhism." The other is *Zen*, with its curious, unanswerable questions.

In the early days of Mahayana Buddhism, its teachers were willing to accept local gods and beliefs in order to get more people to accept the teachings of the Buddha. In this way Buddhism became mixed with animism in some sectors. Animism is a belief in spirits that live in natural things—rocks, fire, water, trees, and the like. These natural spirits may be good or evil.

Animism may be the world's oldest religion. It developed when primitive people observed things in nature that they could not explain. A tree grows, or a rock mysteriously dislodges itself and falls. The quiet air turns into a furious storm. These things had to have a reason for happening. The inquiring mind of early man thought they were caused by spirits within these things.

Tantrism began in India in the seventh century. It was later introduced into Tibet where it is still strong today. Tantrism seeks salvation through chanting *mantras*. Mantras are words and syllables that have no meaning, but which are believed to have a magical effect. One example of a mantra is *Om Ghrur Ghatta ghotaya*.

According to Tantric teaching, a mantra will not work unless fitted to a person or type of person. Uttering the wrong mantra can even be dangerous. Therefore, each person must study under a teacher who can fit the right mantras to the student.

Mantras are not supposed to work unless accompanied by the proper movements of the body, hands, and fingers. These ritual movements are called *mudras*. Each god has his own mudras. A person seeking the god's aid must imitate the god's mudras exactly.

THE YELLOW SECT

The monk-wizard Mar-pa did much to spread Tantric Buddhism in Tibet. Tantrism—differing from the Buddha's beliefs—teaches that human beings have souls. It was said that Mar-pa could detach his soul from his body and enter the body of a dead person.

In time Tibetan Tantrism split into two sects. One is known as the Yellow Sect, the other the Red Sect. They are named for the color of their robes.

The Yellow Sect was founded by Tsong-kha-pa. He wanted to get rid of some of Tantrism's magic and return more closely to the Buddha's original teachings. As leader of the sect, he was called a *lama*, which means "superior one." The name later was applied to all Tantric monks and priests, and the leader was called the Grand Lama. Still later, the leader became the *Dalai Lama. Dalai* in the Mongol language means "ocean" or "great ocean."

The Yellow Sect teaches that the Dalai Lama is reborn as soon as he dies. His soul immediately passes into a baby who is being born. The lesser lamas begin at once to search for him among the newborn boys. There are certain signs they seek to identify the reborn leader, but it is not always easy to find him. In one case they searched for three years.

LEFT-HAND TANTRISM

The magic aspects of Tantrism are in direct conflict with the Buddha's beliefs. He did not believe in spirits or in magic. It is not clear exactly how magic and Buddhism became joined in this sect. As we have seen, Mahayana missionaries, finding it difficult to get people to give up their old beliefs, probably blended Buddhism with local beliefs to get their ideas accepted.

A lacquered wood statue of a Japanese Zen priest, abbot of a monastery, in deep meditation.

It is also likely that part of the mixing came about in an opposite manner. That is, believers in animism and other types of magic-based religions found much to admire in Buddhism and wove its basic principles into their own beliefs.

In a similar way, a curious sect known as Left-Hand Tantrism developed. This sect uses sex as a means toward attaining proper attitudes toward worship. This practice grew directly from some Indian cults of very ancient origin.

Sexual intimacy between men and women outside of marriage was distinctly forbidden by the Buddha and this rule was included in the Precepts. Left-Hand Tantrism argues that the Buddha taught that all actions must be judged according to the intention behind them. Since the motive behind the sexual acts of Left-Hand Tantrism is the attainment of salvation and nirvana, the intention is praiseworthy. Therefore, it is no sin.

ZEN BUDDHISM

Zen is one of the most famous Buddhist sects. It is the form of Buddhism that is most appealing to Western minds. Zen originated in India and was brought to China in the sixth century by the monk Bodhidharma. The Chinese call it *Ch'an*, which means "meditation." *Ch'an* became Zen when it was introduced into Japan.

Meditation has always been a keystone of Buddhism. But Zen teaches that it is everything. Zen followers do not believe in rituals or reading the sutras and do not worship the Buddha or any bodhisattva. Zen does accept the Mahayana belief that all people have a Buddha-nature within themselves. They believe that this buddha-nature can be released only through meditation. Consequently they consider the prayers of Pure Land Buddhism worthless.

In Zen, meditation is more total and intense than in any other Buddhist sect. The Zen follower must avoid all conscious thought except the point upon which he or she is meditating.

There is a famous Zen story about a man who went to a Zen master. He asked to be taught Zen. The Zen master said nothing but began to pour a cup of tea for his visitor, using a cup that was already filled. The extra tea overflowed and ran across the table to drip to the rice-mat-covered floor. Still the Zen master kept pouring until the pot was empty.

Then he spoke at last. "You are like this cup," he said. "You are *full*. How can I pour Zen into you? Empty yourself and come back."

Zen meditation can be practiced by each person on his or her own. However, most seek a teacher to guide them. The teacher provides curious questions for the student to meditate upon. These questions, which are called *koans*, are not supposed to be answered in an ordinary manner. Their purpose is to make one think along a certain line, thus focusing the mind to a single point.

One of the most famous koans is the question: "You can hear two hands clapping, but how can you hear the clap of a single hand?"

Another is: "What makes you answer when you are called?" Still another: "What was your original face—the one you had before your parents gave birth to you?"

"If *nothing* is absolutely nothing, then what is nothingness?" is a koan. So is: "You have climbed to the top of a ten-foot pole. Now how can you climb the rest of the way?"

Let us take the last koan. The obvious answer is that one can climb no higher than the top. The Zen master would reject this answer and send us back to meditate harder.

The question asks us *how* we can climb higher. This implies that there is a way to do it. Our meditating mind ponders the problem. Possible answers are meant to pose new problems. Our mind goes deeper and deeper into the questions. Since our thoughts always reveal our true nature, we are actually digging into our own nature. If we go deep enough, we will finally uncover our own Buddha-nature. Thus, we should find enlightenment within ourselves.

THE ZEN WAY

Zen enlightenment often comes in a sudden burst of inspiration. This does not mean, however, that it comes easy or soon. But when it does come, it is like a sudden burst of light.

We are told of a Zen student who studied for years without achieving enlightenment. Then one very dark night he started to leave the temple. The Zen master gave him a lantern with a candle inside. The student bowed his thanks and turned to go. The master stopped him, took back the lantern, and blew out the candle flame. He then handed the dark lantern back to the student.

In that instant the startled student became enlightened.

The master had decided that the student had all the instruction he needed. He was being held back because he was depending upon his teacher. He should have been seeking answers to his questions within himself. Blowing out the candle symbolized the need to find one's own way. The act removed the blinds from the student's eyes. At long last he saw his own nature and the way to salvation.

BUDDHISM TODAY

Today, Buddhism is the world's fourth largest religion. Christianity, with its many denominations, is the world's largest with approximately 955 million followers. Islam is second with 538 million. Hinduism is third with 525 million. Buddhists are estimated at 250 million. The vast majority of Buddhists live in Asia but there are also 222,000 in Europe, 190,000 in South America, 16,000 in Oceania (Pacific Ocean area), and 2,000 in Africa.

North America has 150,300 Buddhists, with the Buddhist Church of America reporting a membership of 60,000 in the United States.

The first entry of Buddhists in any number into the United States occurred when Chinese were imported to California to work as laborers in building the first transcontinental railroad.

Later, the Chinese Exclusion Act, a federal law barring entry of Orientals into the United States, cut off immigration for many years. However, Orientals continued to immigrate to Hawaii, which did not become United States territory until 1898. Thus, Hawaii became the largest Buddhist center in America. Later, California became an important Buddhist stronghold because of the large number of Japanese around Los Angeles and the Chinese in San Francisco.

NON-ORIENTAL BUDDHISTS

Interest in Buddhism was greatly stimulated by the publication of Sir Edwin Arnold's famous book, *The Light of Asia,* in 1879. This was the life of the Buddha told in verse. It brought to many in England and the United States their knowledge of the Buddha's greatness.

Another milestone in making Americans aware of Buddhism's beauty was the World Parliament of Religions. This meeting was held at the Chicago World's Fair in 1893. Here the Theravada monk Anagarika startled many Christians with a lecture in which he compared Buddhism and Christianity. He pointed out how similar their basic teachings are in so many ways.

Books by authorities like Max Müller, Rhys Davids, D. T. Suzuki, Christmas Humphreys, and Edward Conze have likewise helped immeasurably in spreading knowledge of Buddhism to English-speaking peoples.

However, interest in Buddhism was mainly found among intellectuals until after World War II. At that time thousands of young American men were stationed in Japan, Korea, Taiwan, and later in Thailand. Many were influenced by Buddhism during their overseas duty tours. Also, thousands of Japanese, Korean, and Chinese war brides entered the United States, which helped swell the number of Buddhists in this country.

SOCIAL CHALLENGES TO BUDDHISM

Back in its Asian strongholds, Buddhism is facing strong challenges as it becomes involved in the social changes of today's world.

Except in Sri Lanka, where monks have always taken part in politics, Buddhism in the past has been content to stay out of the government. This is changing. In Burma the socialistic government in power is trying to base its policies upon Buddhist ideals. Tibet, governed until 1959 by the Dalai Lama as priest-king, is now controlled by China. Although the government is Communist, there is no indication that the religion is being disturbed. Vietnam is also Communist, after a long and bloody civil war. It is too early to tell what effect this will have upon the Buddhist church there.

The takeover by the Communist Khmer Rouge government in Cambodia has been disastrous to the Buddhist church there. Opposition to the religious order was growing in Cambodia even before the Communist takeover. This was because Cambodia is a poor country. It supported seventy thousand professional monks and about thirty thousand young men who took the robe as a religious obligation for six months. This removed one hundred thousand men from the work force. At the same time, they had to be supported with food and shelter. Liberal groups attacked them as "nonproductive" and accused the Buddhist church of resisting social change. This opposition has greatly increased under the Khmer Rouge government.

BUDDHISM AND COMMUNISM

The basic ideas of Communism and Buddhism are opposed to each other. Communism teaches that labor produces a nation's wealth, but that working people do not receive a fair share for their work. This leads to a "class struggle" in which labor strives to gain a fair share of what it produces. Communism will use revolution and violence to achieve its goals.

The Buddha rejected wealth, while Communism wants to redistribute it. He rejected violence, and saw no reason for fighting against the world's ills. They were caused by bad karma and nothing could be done about that, except to work for salvation. The benefits that Communism seeks are things that the Buddha claimed only add to humanity's cravings, and these, in turn, hinder salvation.

BUDDHISM AND CHINESE COMMUNISM

Despite these great differences, it appears possible for Buddhism and Communism to coexist. They seem to be doing so in China. China, of course, is a Mahayana country. Mahayana monks and priests work for their living. Therefore, the charge of nonproductiveness cannot be leveled against Buddhists in China, as it can in Cambodia. In fact, the Chinese Ch'an sect has a slogan, "One day no work, one day no food." They do not live by begging as Theravada monks do.

The Chinese government insists that it permits religious freedom, but admits that religion is not encouraged. During the 1950s there was an attempt to revise Buddhist doctrine to include Communist ideas. Special schools were set up to provide Communist-trained administrators for the temples and monasteries. A new temple was built in Peking to house the tooth of the Buddha preserved in China. Cultural exchanges between Chinese Buddhists and foreign Buddhists were encouraged.

Then, suddenly, all temples were closed during the Cultural Revolution that swept China in 1966. This was not necessarily an attack upon the church. All China was in a turmoil because of a power struggle within the government.

In 1972 temples were reopened. Attempts were again made to contact foreign Buddhist groups. Even more important, the central Chinese government began emphasizing the great contributions Buddhism had made to Chinese culture in art, literature, and philosophy.

This is heartening to Buddhists everywhere. It indicates that

Communism is beginning to appreciate the religion. However, visitors to China point out that lay membership seems to be falling. In the temples, visitors see monks going about their duties undisturbed by the government, but the crowds of lay worshipers no longer jam the courtyards as they once did. Some observers worry that Buddhism in China may become a religion for monks rather than for ordinary people. This is already true for the most part in Theravada countries today.

BUDDHISM IN MODERN INDIA

Buddhists everywhere are interested in the revival of their religion in India. This is because India is the home of the Buddha and the birthplace of Buddhism.

While writers claim there is a revival of Buddhism there, it is very small. Mostly it is Theravada, inspired by the missionary work of the Maha Bodhi Society of Sri Lanka. Mahayana Buddhism is represented in India almost entirely by Tibetan exiles. They came to India when their Dalai Lama fled from the Chinese invasion in 1959. One of the reasons Mahayana Buddhism is having trouble reviving in India is that over the years Hinduism has taken into itself many Buddhist ideas. The difference between popular Hinduism and popular Buddhism is no longer as great as it once was.

YOUTH AND VIOLENCE

Buddhism is not a religion that changes much. The majority of the major sects follow their old doctrines. This reliance on tradition is bringing Buddhism into conflict in some countries with the increasing violence of the day. For example, in Laos, Vietnam, and Cambodia,

A sixth-century bronze Indian Buddha.

A young man, joining a monastery in Thailand for three months, puts on his saffron robe. His student uniform hangs on the wall.

the values of Buddhism are opposed to the violent political upheavals of recent years.

The situation is somewhat different in Thailand. Thailand is the only country in Southeast Asia to keep its independence when European nations were building colonial empires around the world.

Social pressure in Thailand has always been strong, requiring every young man to spend his three to six months in a monk's robe. In rural areas one who has not done so is not considered a desirable person. Some families will not accept him as a son-in-law. Some will not employ him. In the larger cities this attitude is not as strict as it once was.

Universal service as a monk is one of the reasons why Thailand has had very little internal trouble in the past. The country underwent a number of revolutions. But these were almost bloodless in the twentieth century. They were little more than a forced change of government.

But the situation in Thailand has changed in the last four years. Violent and bloody student riots in Bangkok, the capital, have overthrown two governments and threaten the present one. The demand for social changes is starting to prove stronger than the Buddhist concept of enduring the world's miseries and looking to nirvana for final peace.

BUDDHISM'S FUTURE

The awakening of interest in Buddhism in India and the West does not change the larger picture very much. The bulk of the world's Buddhists continue to live in eastern Asia. In Japan, Taiwan, Nepal, and Mongolia followers of the religion are expected to continue their age-old ways. In China and Cambodia, the future is uncertain. Buddhism in Communist countries will be influenced by the governments' attitude toward it.

However, Buddhist scholars point out that any drastic effect Communism may have on Buddhism will be temporary. In the patient East "temporary" can be a very long time. Several times, they say, Buddhism came under state control in China. This happened particularly in the fourth and eighth centuries. But it always made an independent comeback later. They point to the words of the Buddha:

"In the end Truth will always triumph."

"And what is Truth?" a Buddhist scholar asked. We have only to look to the Buddha's first sermon for the answer:

"There is no savior in the world except Truth. Have confidence in the Truth, even though you may not comprehend it; although its sweetness may seem bitter. Trust in the Truth. None can alter it. None can improve it."

After the Buddha spoke these words, those listening cried joyfully:

"The Blessed One has set the Wheel of Truth rolling. No one god or man can ever turn it back. Truth will be preached upon the earth. It will spread, bringing righteousness, goodwill, and peace to mankind."

IMPORTANT DATES IN BUDDHIST HISTORY

Ancient history dates are not exact. Scholars fail to agree on them. Even the Buddha's birth date is an educated guess. Therefore, all dates should be considered as approximate for times before A.D. 1000.

1500 B.C. Aryan tribes invade India, later deifying their leaders in the Hindu religion. Caste system introduced.
563 B.C. Birth of Siddhartha Gautama, the future Buddha.
534 B.C. Prince Siddhartha leaves his home to seek enlightenment.
528 B.C. Siddhartha becomes the Buddha and preaches his first sermon in a deer park near Banaras. This sermon introduced the Four Noble Truths and the Eightfold Path.
483 B.C. Death of the Buddha and his entry into nirvana.
383 B.C. Sects begin to form which led to formation of Mahayana Buddhism.
273 B.C. Birth of Asoka, who later organized Buddhist missionaries.
240 B.C. Asoka introduces Buddhism to Ceylon (Sri Lanka).

A.D. 100 Buddhism becomes popular in China.
384 Buddhism introduced into Korea.
551 Indian missionaries establish Buddhism in Burma.
552 Korean missionaries carry Buddhism to Japan.
700 Tantric Buddhism introduced into Tibet.
800 Buddhism begins to merge with Hinduism in India.
997 Suryavarman II introduces Buddhism into Cambodia and Southeast Asia.
1519 Conquest of India by Mogul Baber practically ends Buddhism in India. Buddhism has been on the decline.
1946 Communist victory in China greatly affects Buddhism in that country.
1950 World Fellowship of Buddhists meets in Ceylon (Sri Lanka), adopts Theravada name for older Hinayana sect.
1957 Buddhist world observes 2500th anniversary of the Buddha's birth.
1959 Chinese invasion of Tibet ends rule of the Dalai Lama, Tibetan priest-king. The Dalai Lama fled to India where his fellow exiles participated in a revival of Mahayana Buddhism in the land of the Buddha's birth.
1966 Buddhist temples closed in China due to Cultural Revolution.
1972 Buddhist temples reopened in China.
1978 World Buddhists number over 249 million members.

GLOSSARY

ascetics—Those who believe that fasting and punishing the flesh will lead to enlightenment.
atman—The Hindu word for human soul.
Avalokitesvara—(uv-ā-*low*'-key-tash-ver-ā) A Mahayana god of great mercy. The name means "the Lord who looks down."
avatar—A god reborn on earth in human form.
Bhagavan—"The Blessed One." A name for the Buddha.
bodhisattva—(*bow*'-dee-sat-whu) An enlightened one who is just below a Buddha; also, a person destined to be a Buddha.
Buddha—"The Enlightened One." Used with the article *the*, it means Siddhartha Gautama, founder of Buddhism. Used with the article *a*, it means any other enlightened person.
Dalai Lama—Spiritual leader of the Tibetan Yellow Sect.
dharma—(*dur*'muh or *dah*-rmuh) Spiritual law based upon the Buddha's teachings.
enlightenment—When a Buddhist is freed from craving for worldly things. He or she is then free from rebirth and can enter nirvana.
guru—Hindu word for teacher.

kalpa—(*kul*-pay) An incredibly long period of time. The age of a world.
karma—(*car'*-muh) The effect of a person's good and bad deeds during his or her lifetime. Karma causes rebirth.
koan—Odd questions used in Zen Buddhism to direct a student's thoughts.
lama—A Tibetan Buddhist priest.
Mahayana—"The Great Vehicle." The largest of the two main divisions of Buddhism.
mantras—Magical words or syllables used in Tantric Buddhism.
meditation—Deep, personal religious thought.
moksha—Release of the Hindu soul to rejoin Brahma the creator.
mudras—Mystic movements that must accompany the chanting of magical mantras in Tantric Buddhism.
nirvana—(nir-*vah'*-nuh) The spiritual place of supreme happiness where a Buddhist goes after enlightenment.
reincarnation—Rebirth of a person after death into a new life.
Sakyamuni—"Sage of the Sakya Tribe." A name for the Buddha.
sangha—Community of Buddhist monks and nuns.
Siva—One of the Hindu trinity of gods. The Destroyer.
sutras—Sermons; particularly those of the Buddha.
Tantrism—A Buddhist sect that uses magic rituals.
Theravada—"Doctrine of the Elders." Second largest Buddhist division. Formerly called Hinayana.
Zen—A Buddhist sect that emphasizes meditation.

SUGGESTIONS FOR FURTHER READING

Cohen, Joan O.
Buddha.
New York: Delacorte Press, 1969.

Garland, Patricia W. (with Dunstan, Mary Jane).
Orange-Robe Boy.
New York: Viking Press, 1967.

Kalem, Betty.
Gautama Buddha in Life and Legend.
New York: Lothrop, Lee & Shepard, 1969.

Life Magazine, editorial staff.
The World's Great Religions.
New York: Simon & Schuster, 1958.

Serage, Nancy.
The Prince Who Gave Up a Throne.
New York: Crowell, 1966.

INDEX

Anagarika, 49
Ananda, 16, 26
Angkor Thom, 35
Angkor Wat, 30
Animism, 28, 42, 45
Arnold, Sir Edwin, 49
Aryans, 4
Asceticism, 7, 21
Ashvaghosha, 2
Asoka, Emperor, 27
Atman, 11
Avalokitesvara, 35
Avatar, 4

Bhagavan. *See* Buddha (Prince Siddhartha Gautama)
Bodhidharma, 45
Bodhisattvas, 33, 35, 39
Borodudur temple, 30

Brahma (god), 4, 7, 10, 11
Buddha (Prince Siddhartha Gautama)
   asceticism and, 7, 21
   death of, 26
   early life, 2
   first sermon, 13
   Hinduism and, 1, 4, 6, 10, 11
   Jataka Tales, 23, 25–26
   karma and, 6, 10, 11–12, 15
   meditation and, 8, 9
   nirvana and, 10–11, 22
   sangha, 15–17, 18, 21
   studies of, 6
   See also Buddhism
Buddha Amida (Amitabha), 40
Buddha illusions, 38
Buddhacarita ("Acts of the Buddha"), 2

Buddhism
- Asoka and, 27
- Communism and, 50–52, 56
- dharma, 17, 21, 22–23
- Eightfold Path, 13, 15, 22
- Four Noble Truths, 8, 9, 13, 22, 36
- future of, 55
- magic, 42–43, 45
- Mahayana, 31, 33, 35–39, 42, 43, 51, 52
- Middle Way, 21–22
- missionaries, 27–28
- nirvana, 1, 10–11, 22, 36
- persecution, 28
- Precepts, 17–18, 36
- Pure Land, 39–40, 45
- reincarnation, 6, 10, 12
- social challenges to, 49–50, 52–55
- spread of, 28, 30
- Tantrism, 42–43, 45
- Theravada, 31, 33, 35–36, 52
- in United States, 48, 49
- Zen, 45–47
- See also Buddha (Prince Siddhartha Gautama)

Burma, 30, 50

Cambodia, 30, 50, 52, 55
China, 2, 30, 45, 50–53, 56
Christianity, 48, 49
Communism, 50–52, 56
Conze, Edward, 49
Creation, 37

Dalai Lama, 43, 50, 52
Davids, Rhys, 49
Description of the Happy Land, 30
Dharma, 17, 21–23
Dravidian Indians, 4

Eightfold Path, 13, 15, 22
Enlightenment, 1, 8, 9, 47

Four Noble Truths, 8, 9, 13, 22, 36

Genesis, book of, 37

Hinayana Buddhism. *See* Theravada Buddhism
Hinduism, 1, 4, 6–7, 10, 11, 28, 48, 52
Humphreys, Christmas, 49

India, 1, 2, 27, 28, 45, 52

Indonesia, 30
Indra (god), 4
Islam, 28, 30, 48

Japan, 2, 30, 39–40, 45, 49, 55
Jataka Tales of the Buddha, 23, 25–26, 39
Jehovah, 40
Jesus Christ, 38

Kalpa, 37–38
Karma, 6, 10, 11–12
Koans, 46
Korea, 2, 30, 49

Laos, 2, 43, 52
Left-Hand Tantrism, 45
Light of Asia, The (Arnold), 49
Lion's skin, story of the, 23, 25
Lotus of the Good Law, 36, 38

Magic Buddhism, 42–43, 45
Maha Bodhi Society of Sri Lanka, 52
Mahayana Buddhism, 31, 33, 35–39, 42, 43, 51, 52
Malaya, 30
Manjusri, 33
Mantras, 42

Mara the Tempter, 8–9
Mar-pa, 43
Meditation, 8, 9, 45–47
Middle Way, 21–22
Missionaries, 27–28
Moksha, 6–7, 10
Mongolia, 2, 55
Mudras, 42
Muhammad, 28
Müller, Max, 49
Mustard seed, story of the, 25–26

Nagasena, 11
Nepal, 55
Nirvana, 1, 10–11, 22, 36
Nuns, 16–17

Pali canon, 2
Precepts, 17–18, 36
Pure Land Buddhism, 39–40, 45

Questions of King Milinda, The (Nagasena), 11

Rahula, 2
Red Sect (Tantrism), 43
Reincarnation, 6, 10, 12
Ryonen, 17

Sakyamuni. *See* Buddha (Prince Siddhartha Gautama)
Sangha, 15–18, 21
Siddhartha Gautama, Prince. *See* Buddha (Prince Siddhartha Gautama)
Siva (god), 4, 28
Sivaism, 28
Sri Lanka, 2, 28, 49
Suryavarman I, King, 30
Suzuki, D. T., 49

Taiwan, 49, 55
Tantrism, 42–43, 45
Thailand, 2, 30, 49, 55
Theravada Buddhism, 31, 33, 35–36, 52

Tibet, 2, 30, 42, 43, 50
Tsong-kha-pa, 43

United States, 48, 49

Vietnam, 2, 50, 52
Vishnu (god), 4

Wheel of Life, 6, 10, 38
Women, in sangha, 16–17
World Parliament of Religions (1893), 49

Yellow Sect (Tantrism), 43

Zen Buddhism, 45–47

ABOUT THE AUTHOR

I. G. Edmonds is the author of more than thirty books for young readers on topics in history, biography, and Middle Eastern affairs. His home base is in California with his family, but he travels widely and at regular intervals, most often to the Middle and Far East. He is also the author of *Islam*, another title in the Franklin Watts First Book series.

J
294.3
E

Edmonds

Buddhism.

78 8183 84
88 85
98

cc 14, 1981 ed.

HAYNER PUBLIC LIBRARY DISTRICT

Alton, Illinois

OVERDUES 5¢ PER DAY. MAXIMUM FINE
COST OF BOOKS. LOST OR DAMAGED BOOKS
ADDITIONAL $2.00 SERVICE CHARGE.